IN MY DREAMS I'M DANCING

©Ruth Wood
2008

ISBN 978-1-4092-3669-6

THOUGHTS FROM A WHEELCHAIR

So here I am, sitting in the middle of the tools section in B&Q. This is not my preferred place. In fact on a scale of 1 to 10 I would give it about minus 90. But I don't have much choice.

Since I have been in a wheelchair, I have discovered just how very differently men shop as opposed to women. When my carer/chauffeur spots a well stocked tools section, he virtually salivates. In fact, he has all the appearance of a woman in a designer dress shop with the word SALE emblazoned across every rack. I have looked at the drills/screwdrivers/whatever that he is handling with a slightly glazed expression and in the past I have said things like "haven't you got two of those already" and he has said, with a look of incredulity that I could so misunderstand what is going on, "not like this one, no" and I would give up and go and look at the lighting section (I never buy any, I just like to look). Well, that was the past. There's no point saying anything now, partly because he is well over 6 feet tall and I am reduced to the level of a pushchair, but also because he has parked me out of the way and wandered off, so he wouldn't hear me anyway.

Now don't get me wrong. This man has a virtual halo around his lovely head for the way he has been looking after me since I came out of hospital. But I am realising more and more that's it's not so much a question of women come from Venus and men come from Mars, more a sort of men hunt and gather and buy tools and women do their own thing.

Just before we came in here, we went to a shopping centre – all on the ground floor, disabled toilets (or toilets for the disabled – but it was locked anyway) and every shop only disabled friendly because they can move all the displays that are on wheels. Now I am fairly shy – especially with people I don't know – and even shyer about "making a scene (very "English") – and my preferred method when shopping in a new store is to have a quick gander through the window, decide if they've got the kind of thing I want, suss out how the shop's arranged, then quietly walk in and look around. I never make a fuss and I rarely ask a shop assistant for – well – assistance. What I do not want to do – other than in my worst nightmares – is to be pushed straight into the shop, knocking aside display racks, catching small children on the ankles and forcing the shop assistant to rush over and move all the fittings – even the ones people are looking at. If I had ever wanted this amount of attention I would have found a job jumping out of birthday cakes half naked at all-male parties. But this is what happened in the bag shop. And I can't communicate with my driver because he's way above my head and behind me – and anyway he's deaf and won't wear his hearing aid. The worst bit about all this is that the shop didn't sell what I was looking for anyway – something I would have quickly realised if I'd had time to look through the window. Eventually I made my feelings known (by shouting "they haven't got what I want) and we left.

Of course, another thing about a wheelchair – even the nice one I'm in – is that your feet stick out of the front. My feet are not huge – a narrow size six and a half and quite dainty – but they still jut forward of the footrests. As I found out in Boots when I was pushed straight up to the counter. I know

I've not got much feeling in my feet anyway, but it's the principle of the thing.
Having educated my carer/chauffeur in this delicate point, in the next shop he parked me sideways on to the displays.

Which is why I'm sitting in B&Q with a cricked neck.

I feel as if my life has gone down the wrong end of a telescope. One minute every day is full of exciting things, a job, travel, a good social life and a shiny new husband, then suddenly it's zoomed down to total dependence on other people, inability to even tie a shoelace (I haven't got any but if I did I couldn't do it) and being pushed where I may not necessarily want to go. I'm used to towering over people (I'm 5 foot 10), helping get cans down from shelves in supermarkets for tiny little old ladies, and suddenly here I am at everyone's crotch level and eye to eye with small children in pushchairs. And I'm crowd phobic (an extension of my claustrophobia – note the panic attack when they tried to give me an MRI scan).

Now don't get me wrong – I'm not whinging and whiny – well not most of the time anyway. But I feel a bit like Alice in Wonderland – I've fallen down a rabbit hole and my whole life has completely changed. One minute I'm getting over a virus attack, next I can't walk and am in hospital with TM. (More of that later)

Now the hospital was quite interesting. I have to say straight away that the staff were superb (especially during the night one of the male patients lost it and had to be restrained by two male nurses) and everything was cleaned every day.

The first few days of my incarceration I really wasn't aware of very much – which was probably just as well. Then they took me down for the MRI (the previously mentioned panic attack) which was a bit of a shock and only lasted about 30 seconds before they had to pull me out and calm me down. A couple of days later they filled me up with happy pills and put me in the machine again, and it suddenly became quite a nice experience (a policy I have followed ever since). I had my eyes shut and the background hum became the engines of a large, sleek ship; the repeated louder noises were the sounds of waves lapping against the boat (it was one of the best holidays I've never had).

Next day after a delicious lunch (I have to say the food was excellent) came the "little test" otherwise known as a lumbar puncture. I will say very little about this, other than the fact I would rather have any number of babies without anaesthesia than have that again. We pass rapidly on.

After the diagnosis (more later – I'll give you plenty of warning so you can skip that bit) came treatment time. Strictly speaking there's no cure – but they have a way of zonking the inflammation (in the spine – more later in the boring bit) with large amounts of steroids given intravenously over three days. Great fun – you can feel it creeping up your arm. And what made it even better was on day three when they informed me there were no drip stands available (only two for the whole ward) so they hung it on the curtain rail round my bed. Very third world.

I was in hospital for three weeks, during which time they moved my bed to different bays four times. I didn't mind the change of scene, or the fact that at one point I ended up next to a batty old dear who kept showing my get well cards to her visitors and said she was coming home with me, but it was such a pain having to tell my friends that my phone number had changed.

For those of you fortunate enough not to have been near a hospital in the last ten years, they now have a combined telephone/television over every bed. You have to pay (of course), but it's really nice to be able to sit and gossip – keeps you in touch with the real world outside and you can even go online and get your e-mails. Every screen has its own telephone number – and therein lies the problem. More than one of my friends was startled to be greeted by a male voice when they thought they were phoning me (it was a mixed ward).

I also received daily visits from two physiotherapists (when I jokingly referred to them as physioterrorists, they smiled in a benign way that informed me that if they could have a pound for every time they heard that particular variation, they wouldn't be working for the national health any more). They gave me some very simple exercises – I could do these standing on my head! Only trouble was, when I tried to do them, my body just didn't want to know. The spirit was willing but the body had gone on strike. I became very frustrated, and in a fit of depression, sent an e-mail to my son telling him about it. The reply I got back kept me chuckling for days. "Mum", it said, "if at first you don't succeed, find out what the loser gets".

I came out just before Christmas, and due to the fact that I couldn't do much other than lie in bed and stagger to the loo, the festive season didn't really happen. Mind you, I made it to my son's wedding in Scotland at the end of December – amazing what you can do when you're determined – and it was challenging to find ways to hide my crutches and unflattering black slip-ons during the photos. Most of the time I hid behind the bride's dress, which worked quite well.

Anyway, here comes the end of my musings – himself has torn himself away from the tools and is preparing to launch me into the next chapter of adventure.

(note to self – try to obtain a self-propelling wheelchair as soon as possible)

REHABILITATION

When I told my son I was going into rehab, I thought he'd never stop laughing (this is the one who, when I went into hospital to have a broken nose sorted out, told everyone his mother was having a "nose job"). After three months of coping (or not!) at home, I have received a letter instructing me to be ready on Thursday mornings between 8.15 am and 9.45 (there's an 8.15 in the morning?!) when an ambulance will collect me and deliver me to the local hospital, leave me for two hours, then collect me again. So on this, my first morning, my CC helps me get up early (for me) and gets my breakfast ready at 7.30. I can't really eat at that time of the morning, but I do my best. I've opted to wear jogging bottoms (now there's an irony!) and a loose T-shirt – apart from covering my flabby bits, I can remember the exercises I was given in the hospital, and a skirt is simply not appropriate.

I'm ready and waiting by 8.00, my excitement mounting (well, hey, I don't get out much). By 9.00 my CC suggests making me another cup of tea. I decide not to risk it – I'm sure the ambulance will arrive at any minute. At 9.30 I agree. At 9.45 I'm seriously worried that I've got the day wrong, or they've forgotten me. I'm just looking up the number on the letter, when they arrive outside.

It's a bit of a palaver getting me plus my wheelchair into the ambulance. However, once in they latch the chair onto a couple of metal bars on the floor, strap me in, and we're off.

There are another couple of ladies already seated, and we say our hellos. They start chatting to each other, they have obviously met before, and I'm quite happy to listen to their conversation. The ambulance man sitting near me is watching me, and starts to ask me about my "condition". I'm a bit reluctant to go into it at first, but he seems genuinely interested, and soon we're chatting happily. When we get to the hospital, I'm almost sorry to have to get off.

Inside, I'm wheeled into a large room, subdivided by curtains. I'm to discover that different groups are allocated different areas, and the noise transfer makes life extremely difficult – especially when, as today, the MS group are trying to have a relaxation session at the same time as one of the OTs is interviewing an extremely deaf man. The atmosphere is not very conducive to anyone relaxing.

I have my initial interview, and am given a red book in which to keep all my details. I'm then handed over to the neuro-physio, a very nice but obviously stressed woman. She wheels me over to some parallel bars. Just for a moment I'm consumed by flights of fancy – I've seen those athletes using these, swinging effortlessly up onto their hands, their bodies poised to take wing. Heigh ho. It's all I can do to stagger out of the chair and haul myself along a few paces. Exhaustion sets in and I have to sit down again. I'm taken to an area where another lady is already sitting and we make small talk until it's time to go home again. I'm a bit disappointed I haven't been given any specific exercises, but I assume that will come later.

As the weeks go by, I begin to enjoy the drive there and back – the ambulance men (mainly men, I only saw one woman) are very chatty. The rehab itself is not quite what I had expected. I am still not given exercises specific to my condition. The small group of people I am with all have different problems – we seem to be the ones that can't be fitted in anywhere else. For a while I travel back and forth with a girl with MS, who talks about the "mandatory cup of tea" we all have on arrival. After a couple of weeks I am advised to give up caffeine, so even that small pleasure is denied me. And I hate water – as far as I'm concerned it's lovely to look at in a pond or fountain, and wonderful when it's hot and full of bubbles as I lie in my bath with a glass of champagne (oh ok that last bit's pretend, but you know what I mean) but to actually put it in your mouth and swallow it? No way Jose. So I go without (cue for sigh).

The day has come when it is decided that I no longer need to travel by ambulance. I am now struggling along on two crutches, so the rehab unit's own ambulance is sent to collect me, together with another man who is in a wheelchair. I must admit, I don't really enjoy the journey any more. The two ladies who transport us know each other very well – apparently grew up together locally – so their conversation is only to each other and excludes anyone else. I take to glumly staring out of the window.

Although I don't get much in the way of proper exercises, just spend a bit of time walking up and down between parallel bars (and they put a full length mirror on the wall so you can see yourself struggling – how gross is that), sometimes they do quite interesting things. Today a member of staff has put a box on the table in front of me, with one end open and the other covered by a cloth. She explains to me that I will put my hand inside the box through the curtain, she will put something on my palm and I then have to see if I can identify it by touch alone. This is to give her some idea as to how extensive the area of insensitivity is in my hands, but I find it really hard to get up the courage. Who knows what she will put in my mitt (those of you with brothers will understand!)

The first object is a total mystery – I can tell it's hard, but whether it's wood or plastic – no idea. I turn it round, and discover a long groove running down its length. Nope. I admit defeat and am allowed to look at it. It's a peg. (Try this at home if you want) Anyway, after this I lose enthusiasm for this sort of activity (I'm not a very good loser, which is quite surprising considering the way I play cards).

NEW WHEELCHAIR

A month before all this exciting activity, my parents had bought me a wheelchair. The one I started with was hired from the red cross, and had to go back after a month. My GP had put in a request for an NHS wheelchair, but it was turned down because I didn't "need it in the house". (The mere fact that you can't get a wheelchair into my house unless it's folded up didn't seem to count – I suppose the powers that be don't know about small cottages where there are pieces of furniture to hold on to every two paces or so) So one day my Mum phoned up and said "we're going to buy you a wheelchair. Now don't argue" (I had no intention of doing so) "what would you like?" And – you've guessed it – the first words that came out of my mouth were, "self propelling". So a couple of weeks later we took delivery of a beautiful black and chrome chair called "Enigma". Wonderful. What was good enough for Elgar was good enough for me!

It starts well. My carer/chauffeur finds it easier to push than the previous monstrosity – cue for faster walking. I need a safety belt. I need a crash hat. I need to do it for myself. So – into a garden centre. He stops at books (nearly as much a lure as tools). I say "see you" and begin to "spin the wheels". Now when I'd asked for this type of wheelchair I hadn't taken into account that my palms and fingers are permanently painful – so time to grit the teeth. No gain without pain – or in this case independence. I trundle in a determined manner up one aisle, down another then stop for a rest in front of the fish tanks. As I contemplate the peaceful sight of a large number of striped fish darting in a maniacal fashion around the glass, there suddenly appears the dreaded shop assistant. "There you are" she says "you're husband's looking for you. Let me help you" and before I have time to say farewell to my fishy companions (they didn't miss me – we hadn't had time to bond) I get whisked away by this total stranger. She wheels me up to my CC with a jolly, "here we are then". I almost expect her to ask him to sign for me. Off she goes. I can hardly speak. overcome as I am with emotion (have you ever wanted to strangle two people simultaneously, one of them a complete stranger – not easy to execute but I was willing to give it a try) and my beloved one says, "I asked her if she'd seen a wheelchair 'cos I'd lost you".

My rage is complete.

INCONSTANCY

I'm sitting in a large waiting area trying not to look at the gruesome pictures on the walls. I don't know who they're meant for, but did they need to be in full colour? And labelled? Whose idea was this? Still, it temporarily takes my mind off the impending consultation.

I take a quick look at my chauffeur. He's leafing through a three year old copy of Cosmopolitan. I hope it's not the one with details of female orgasms – he might get ideas.

We've already established he's not coming in with me. Not this time. Much too embarrassing.

I received the summoning letter last week; discreet brown envelope – the postman probably thought it was a mucky mag. It was from yet another healthcare professional – this one's title under her signature was "continence advisor".

Now one of the many untalked-about aspects of my condition is a certain problem known as an "overactive bladder". When I was a child, I was accused of having an overactive imagination ("Ruth has an overactive imagination") but this is new. When it began happening I was mortified. I wheeled myself into Boots and sat in front of the display between sanitary towels and babies nappies. There was a bewildering array, different "absorbencies", some with wings (!), I had no idea. So I decided to get three different types and use trial and error.

Do you know how difficult it is to conceal the contents of your shopping basket when you're in a wheelchair and it's on your lap? As I sat in the queue I felt everyone around me looking down into my basket and knowing my little problem. My cheeks were burning, and once I got out I decided to get more online (thank goodness for the internet). (Later I found the Tena website which sends you free samples to try and explains everything.)

As I sit here, avoiding making eye contact with the walls, I begin to speculate whether or not a continence advisor ever tells anyone what she/he does. I mean, can you just imagine at a dinner party, somewhere between the soup and the curry "what do you do for a living?" "oh, I'm a continence advisor". End of conversation. It's much worse than being a singing teacher (like me). All I get is people telling me they can't sing a note, but have always wanted to try, but they bet I can't teach them. (My response always veers from "everyone can sing" on a good day when I'm prepared to take part in spirited discussion, to "probably not then" when I'm bored and want to go home). Of course, nobody asks what I do any more. I'm defined by my disability now, not my occupation.

My name is called. Everyone else watches to see which door I'm going through. Ok, so now about 40 people know I've got bladder problems.

I get asked the usual questions (birth date, address, easy stuff) then have an ultra sound exam. I'm quite pleased about this. I was always slightly envious when my daughter had these when she was pregnant; I don't think they were around in my child bearing part of life. Unlike my daughter, I'm not offered copies of the pictures to take home (now there's a subject for dinner parties – reach into purse – "oh do have a look at my bladder, isn't it wonderful?" sighs of envy all round).

Dressed, back to my seat. Now the difficult questions. I have no idea whether my "stream" is any different now than before the illness. It's not something I've ever thought about – added to which I can't really feel much now anyway. I'm given the good news that I'm not "retaining urine" – oh boy, this is getting very basic. The last time I had a conversation like this, I was 8 and being teased because the girl in the next cubicle could hear me tinkling. So I would not need to "catheterise" – this is going from bad to worse. We discuss pelvic floor – mine's usually very strong thank you, after all, I am a singing teacher. No, apparently I've lost power in this part of my anatomy. I'm liking this less and less (and I wasn't very happy to start with). Then comes the ultimate indignity – given a glass vial and a cardboard container and wheeled off to the ladies to do a sample. As I emerge from the room, chauffeur looks up from his Cosmo and says, "are you finished then?" beginning to get up. Everyone looks round. I mutter "no" and make sort of flapping motions at him with my hand. He sits down again, looking bewildered. I look straight ahead as I'm wheeled between the chairs and round the corner – I know if I looked even the garish pictures on the walls would be leering at me.

Later, back in the "continence" room, I'm told there's a drug to treat my "problem". Oh good. But I must abstain from any caffeine or alcohol. Not so good. And there are side effects. Apparently I will get a very dry mouth. And possibly a headache. Oh, wonderful. So now I wake up with a hangover without having had the fun bit first. I go home via the supermarket, where chauffeur buys caffeine-free tea and coffee. I'm depressed.

A CLEAN MIND IN A?

I've been taking a good look at what is going on in my life, and I've decided one of the things that is depressing me most is the state of the house. I'm not ungrateful for the sterling efforts of my chauffeur/carer, but I can't help feeling that men look at dirt in a different way than women. In fact, I'm not sure that this particular man even *sees* the dirt that I do! Of course, it's not his fault – he was living the life of a bachelor for some twelve years before I moved in, and it's not even as if he's got any daughters, just four sons. One of the first things I did when I got here was to have a new kitchen put in – whilst explaining why having tools, pieces of wood and sundry nuts, screws and bolts on all the kitchen surfaces was not really my idea of hygiene – or a kitchen, come to that. I did compromise – when the new kitchen was finished I put a large wicker basket at one end of the surface (furthest away from food preparation) to put all his "works in progress". The idea was that every month or so he would empty the basket and put the contents away (in logical places like his shed). As a system, it worked quite well for a while, but gradually things began to slip. Now, of course, he's been totally allowed to run riot – I didn't set foot in the kitchen for about two months after I got home from hospital, and before that I was actually in hospital for three weeks, and before that I was ill in bed for three weeks – well, you get the picture. I'd been off the domestic scene for nearly five months, and quite honestly, all was slipping.

Now I must say here that he's very willing and he tries very hard, but everything's against him becoming a domestic god(dess), not least of which is an overabundance of testosterone. So here I am, having persuaded him that we really needed a proper cleaner to come in regularly to help him out. (The final straw came when I watched him vacuum round a sock on the landing for four weeks running. In the end I picked it up – the sock, not the vacuum)

I think he was rather hurt at first, and insisted we "don't need it". He'd thought he was doing a good job – and I must say his ironing skills are phenomenal. Of course, if he shook creases out before he hung up clothes to dry he wouldn't need to iron quite so much – but hey, don't look a gift man in the mouth! However, he couldn't get round the fact that he only hoovered the bits of floor that he could see (and gravity has a habit of catching up with tottering piles of paper), didn't see the point of dusting, couldn't understand why the sheets on the bed needed changing more than once a month, and kept forgetting to clean the loo.

I say no more, but rest my case. We need a cleaner.

So I'm poring over local directories looking for someone suitable.

When I was growing up, we had a huge house (in the days before people wanted big houses so they were relatively cheap) and both my parents were working. So we had a cleaner – well a steady stream actually.

I don't remember much about the first one – she didn't last long. The second one was a very strange person who used to bring her mentally disabled brother with her. He was huge to my young eyes, and sat making mumbling sounds in a chair in the kitchen. Occasionally he would look at me (nervously hovering near the door) and shout "hey" then go quiet again. Very unnerving. His sister (our cleaner) was terrified of the vacuum cleaner, and refused to switch it on. She used to treat it a bit like a duster, running it round the walls, but the floors didn't see much action. One day my mother was at home when she came, and, thinking to be helpful, switched it on. I don't think I've ever seen anyone move so fast – she would have won the 100 metres before anyone else had left the starting point. So she left.

The next one – Mrs M – seemed alright at first. At least she knew how to use all the cleaning utensils, including the vacuum. However, all was not well when my mother found out that Mrs M was bringing her two children with her when she cleaned and feeding them generously from our larder. Anything they couldn't manage they took with them. She was sent packing.

The fourth – and longest serving – was an absolute "treasure". Mrs B interviewed my mother, looked around the house with a critical eye, then announced she'd take the job. She worked two days a week, one half of the house each day, and drank her cup of tea at elevenses standing up. She reigned supreme for some years, and was instrumental in keeping my brother's and my bedrooms tidy ("if you don't tidy up I'll ask Mrs B to do it". The one time I couldn't be bothered, I came home to find all my precious records piled on the bed with the record player on top of them – this was the day of the breakable record. I kept my room tidy thereafter)

So this was my previous experience of employing cleaners. (Mind you, we knew the writing was on the wall the day Mrs B proudly announced that she'd washed that "dirty old painting in the sitting room" with soap and water. It was at the restorers for several weeks. Soap is not recommended for original oils).

I've decided that there is a firm in the directory who might fit the bill – they will remain anonymous. I phone up and make an appointment for the chap who owns the firm to come and see me.

The first intimation I have that maybe this firm is not what I am looking for is when he rings me to say his sat nav can't find me – not just the street but the entire village does not exist (shades of Brigadoon). Sat nav? The firm must be doing well. I find out where he is – actually more or less round the corner. I look out of the front window, and innocently ask "are you driving a black car?" "No" he icily replies, "it's a shogun". Right.

He parks outside and walks up the drive. He is tall, slim, about thirty, wearing a suit and carrying a brief case. A sinking feeling somewhere in my solar plexus recognises that this is going to be expensive.

After he has settled on the settee opposite (actually he perches – I think he's spotted the cat hairs) I explain that I am disabled, my husband is finding everything a bit much and I need someone just to come in once a week,
hoover round and generally clean up. He listens with what I can only describe as a sneer on his face, then asks if he can look round. Which he does. He returns fairly soon (it's a very small house) to give his verdict.

He says he couldn't possibly allow his "girls" to come into the house in the present state. It isn't fair, and they would probably walk out. My jaw drops. He then starts talking about the "wow factor" (I just want my house cleaned, not a tv show) that I would find after his "team of operatives" have come in and done a "complete and in depth clean" (presumably wearing bio-hazard suits and oxygen masks). This would cost me £350. After this, his "girls" would graciously deign to enter my now-pristine home – two every week at a cost of £35 per time.

It's only because my jaw has dropped so far that it takes a lot of effort to fight gravity sufficiently to reclaim it that I don't tell him what I think of him. After a pause, I merely say, "I'm sorry, that's much too much. Good day". I think I probably ruin the rather grand and controlled way I am throwing him out by having to haul myself up from the settee taking three goes to do it. Still, the principle is there.

Back to square one. However, after talking to neighbours, I am able to find a "gem" to be my very own cleaner. T comes once a week for two hours, and is chatty, affable and extremely efficient. My chauffeur/carer has taken to tidying up before she comes (when she looks in "her" cupboard and remarks "someone's been in here" he blanches!) After her first visit, I sit with a contented sigh, and he looks around and says, "now I see what you mean".

It takes a big man to admit he was wrong.

MOBILITY

I've been practicing walking – going up and down stairs (trying to use my leg muscles rather than my arms) and walking to the post box (ok, it's outside the house next door but one – but it's still an achievement!) I'm still not exactly up to marathon distances – even half a marathon – but I couldn't do that even before I got I ill, so I'm not bothered! The best thing is I've graduated away from the wheelchair for short distances.

We went to the local shopping centre recently. I insisted to my chauffeur/carer that I wanted to try out the mobility scheme, and for that he had to park the car in a different car park than usual. Something else I've learned about men – they don't like anything new. He had always parked in Car Park 2, and now I'm insisting he go to Car Park 3. He grumbles a bit, but goes.

I struggle into the mobility place on my two elbow crutches. Before I continue, I must tell you about these crutches. Anyone who's broken a lower limb will understand this bit. These crutches are most ungainly and quite difficult to manoeuvre. When you sit down anywhere, you haven't got a clue what to do with them. In coffee shops they trip up the unwary (usually carrying hot coffee cups) which can be quite spectacular. When travelling in our car, I just sling them on the back seat, but when with friends you have to hang onto them. They're too big to do this comfortably, and get tangled up with the gear lever and the hand brake.

Now I have an extra problem with these crutches (surprise surprise!) in that in addition to my problems in the lower half of my body (more later in the boring bit) I also have problems in my upper half including my arms and hands.

The best way I can describe the hand problem is to give you an exercise (try this at home!). Now, the first thing you do is to tape up the very tips of your fingers in some thick material – wool or leather, anything so long as it prevents you from feeling anything. Now you get a pair of gloves, fill them with stinging nettles and put them on. You keep those on for twenty-four hours. Not keen? OK, I'll let you off. Wish someone could let me off!

Now imagine having to hold onto the hand grips on the crutches, whilst supporting your walking. See my point? Problem.

Still, Rome wasn't built in a day and determination can overcome most things (add your own platitudes here, I've run out). I tried to get some padding for the handles to relieve the pain a little, but the people at rehab didn't have anything suitable. They showed me a catalogue in which they were selling padding specifically for this problem – but as they were over £20 I decided to give that one a miss.

One of the things I've noticed since I became disabled is that as soon as anything is to aid "mobility" – be it a hand rail or an electric scooter – all the prices go up. I think it's probably like buying flowers for Mothering Sunday – all the prices increase to make the most of it. Of course, what makes it even more unacceptable with the mobility aspect is that the vast majority of disabled people are unable to work, and so have very limited resources.

So I discuss this problem with various people, and my father came up trumps. He goes out and buys a load of foam, then spends ages cutting it out and fitting it onto my crutches. It doesn't take away the pressure pain completely, but it certainly helps..

I was talking to my GP recently about this problem. I had the bright idea that surely there must be some kind of anaesthetic cream I could rub onto my hands, and then wear gloves or something. I thought this was an idea I could patent but apparently it doesn't exist. He gave me some paracetomol – I can't take anything stronger because of my ulcer. Heigh ho another good idea gone out of the window.

So here we are in the mobility centre at the shopping centre. There are forms to fill in (a challenge with my hands!) and then I'm offered a rather smart and solid-looking scooter. It even has some velcro ties on it to store my crutches! How cool is that! It has a shopping basket on the front and it's red. The man in the centre gives me a quick run-down on the controls, then takes me outside so I can have a little drive round. When he's satisfied I'm not about to wreck the thing, he lets me loose on the unsuspecting shoppers in the centre.

At first I'm incredibly nervous. I keep reminding myself that until I was struck down (see the boring bit) I was driving a car all over the place with no problem. It doesn't help. This is going to be a steep learning curve.

My chauffeur/carer has been watching all this, and is now walking behind me. I stop. He walks into me. When we sort ourselves out, I say "why are you walking behind me" at the same time he says "why did you stop". I say "because you're walking behind me" at the same time as he says "so I can keep an eye on you". Shoppers avert their gaze and hurry past as the domestic continues. Eventually we start off again. He's still walking behind me.

Now one of the reasons why I had opted for "shop mobility" (as it's called) is so my chauffeur/carer and I can shop together, side by side, like normal people. OK, I know I'm somewhere down near his knees, but it would be an improvement.

We go in single file into Boots – then rapidly out again. There are so many people that I've lost my nerve. It doesn't help that I'm being closely watched by chauffeur/carer (hereon referred to as CC, it's quicker to type). He used to be an observer for Advanced Motorists candidates, so I suppose it's habit. I tell him I'm going off on my own for a while. I know he's just dying to dive into the bookshop, so this makes it easy.

I tootle along fairly happily, getting more confident, but still keeping the speed down. It's a total revelation – if the average pedestrian drove the way they walk there'd be so many accidents all the roads in Britain would be closed. They stop for no apparent reason, suddenly veer in another direction, then slow right down. When they make these manoeuvres, they don't look down to my level – I am to all intents and purposes now invisible. Part of me longs for the days of the wheelchair when at least it was being pushed by a 6 foot 3 inch man with a loud "mind your backs". It might have made me cringe at the time, but at least people (usually) got out of the way.

Small children in pushchairs gaze at me with bewilderment – they're not used to meeting strange adults eye to eye. They crane their heads as I go by. Very odd.

After a while I decide to try a clothes shop. I haven't been shopping for clothes since I got ill. I'm not yet able to go far on my crutches, so I decide to go in on my scooter.

Once inside, I begin to realise my mistake. The aisles are only just wide enough for the scooter and as I struggle on I suddenly become aware of something swinging behind me. I look round and discover to my horror that I've got half the shop hanging off my crutches. I'd got the width of the scooter right, but had failed to take into account the extra width taken up by those wretched crutches strapped on the back. Nobody seems to have noticed – they can't see me beneath all the clothes anyway – so I stop and try to work out what to do. The first thing is to rescue the clothes from the crutches. This goes well. Encouraged I look around to see the most inconspicuous way to replace them. Most of them have been pulled off their hangers, so it's easy enough to see where the clothes came from. But – horror of horrors – I haven't got room to turn round. I'm going to have to *reverse!* Now I don't know about you, but this is a direction I never enjoyed when I was driving. I'm ok reversing when I'm on my own, but all too often some helpful idiot suddenly materialises somewhere to my rear bumper and insists on "waving me in". (I hate to be sexist, but in my experience it's always a male. And I'm blonde and female so I'm on a hiding to nowhere really). It's very difficult for me to stay calm in these circumstances, and before now I have (accidentally) aimed straight at my "helper" who's had to jump out of the way. Well, I've got no-one trying to "help" me now, but it's actually quite difficult to reverse when craning your head round as far as it will go – I'm used to using my mirrors. I tentatively push the lever marked "reverse" and to my horror the scooter starts making a loud "beeping" sound. It's like a lorry going backwards, except without the droned "this vehicle is reversing". I stop again – quickly – and look around. No-one seems to have heard it – for the first time ever I am thankful for the raucous background music. I stop and think. Then it comes to me. Of course. I climb off the scooter, take another look around,

then dump all the clothes on the nearest clothes stand, get back on the scooter and (carefully) edge forwards around a corner, looking nonchalant. (I hope)
By this time I'm feeling so guilty I know I've got to buy something, so I grab the nearest cheap top and start towards the counter.

An assistant leans forwards, eyeballs me and says, "next please" with slight impatience in her voice. I'm rattled, I will admit, and try to manoeuvre this wretched vehicle to the counter. I get it wrong – the handlebars get stuck underneath a display board on the front of the counter. I hand over the top, and hoping she won't notice, start to ease the scooter back. The "beeping" has now become as loud as a symphony orchestra. The notice comes off with a screeching sound. The ground doesn't open up and swallow me, much as I want it to.

The assistant attempts a smile (I think – it might just have been a grimace) and says "don't worry, I'll sort that out". I wait for her to ring up my purchase, handover my card – then realise I can't reach the card reader to put my number in. Unlike some shops, which have the reader on a convenient bit of wire, this one is stuck to the desk. And the scooter is still jammed up against it, so I can't stand up. I do the only thing I can – I get off the scooter on the side away from the counter, then kneel on it to reach the card holder. This works, but the rest of the (rapidly expanding) queue get a good look at my worst side – made even larger by the steroids I'd had pumped into me in the hospital.

The transaction completed, I get back on my scooter, put my card into my handbag and my wrapped top in the basket, then try to get away. The handlebar of the scooter makes a screeching sound as it scrapes all the paint off the front of the counter. I try to make a dignified exit, but unfortunately the effect is rather ruined by the fact that my crutches catch under the arm of a mannequin near the exit, and I've suddenly got an unexpected passenger.

The assistant rushes over, unhooks the mannequin and gives me a very hard stare. I mutter a feeble "sorry" and leave with my dignity in tatters.

FOR MEDICINAL PURPOSES ONLY

I've never been much of a one for tablets, or medicine in general. The odd tablet for a really bad headache and occasional bouts of depression that need treating, but other than that I don't really like them. I remember as a child we had a large cupboard full of various medicines, and every week my mother would dole out some stuff to keep us "regular". We had "stop" medicine and "go" medicine – all fairly basic. Of course, this was in the bad old days before anyone knew about fibre for constipation, and that red wine is good for you.

But here I am looking at a large pile of boxes containing tablets of various sorts. Although my condition has no treatment in its own right (see the boring bit later) I have tablets to treat the exciting side effects (muscle spasms, overactive bladder, not to mention the IBS tablets, and the sleeping tablets, and the tablets for stomach ulcers) and I've got into a sort of routine with them. Some are twice a day, some three times, one half a tablet twice a day (they're minute, so I keep losing the other half) and so forth. Talking of side effects, I've been reading through the various unwanted side effects you can get (sometimes called "contra indications" – why?!) and it's quite scary. It seems that if only one person in the whole world has a problem, then it's printed on the little leaflet inside the box. The weird thing is that so many of them are contradictory ("diorrhea" and "constipation", that sort of thing.) It's probably not a good idea to read these lists – on a par with reading through any medical dictionary – but I've recently been back to my GP to check what's happening and it's turned out to be a side effect of one of the tablets. Then I get another tablet to deal with the side effects of the original tablet and so it could go on. So I'm reading all these lists to make sure that anything that occurs is a side effect. As these lists seem to cover just about everything that could possibly happen to a person's physicality – not to mention mind – I'm just going to assume that everything is a result of the tablets and hope it all settles down eventually.

My CC told me recently about some tablets he's on. He read his little leaflet and amongst the "inform your GP" section was listed, "heart failure". Right.

One of my newer tablets has an effect of reducing appetite which is very good news as far as I'm concerned because I still haven't lost the stone-and-a-half I put on as a result of the steroids I had in the hospital. Trouble is, I can't really take "exercise" at the moment. All the books say that "exercise should elevate your heart rate and leave you slightly breathless". That's me for a trip up the stairs then!

Amongst the side effects (not of the tablets, but the condition (see boring bit later)) is a thing called "spasticity – try saying that fast (or after a medicinal glass of red wine!). I had no idea what was causing it, and it was quite disconcerting.

It began one night a month or so after I came out of hospital. I was lying in bed with my CC (it's ok, he's my husband as well!) having a go-to-sleep cuddle when suddenly my legs started jerking. I kicked CC in the shins – he was understandably bewildered as it would appear he'd done something wrong and I was being aggressive. I reassured him that this was nothing to do with me – my legs were doing it by themselves. It was really odd – the more I tried to stop it, the worse it got. It went on for quite a while, and when it calmed down I was so tired I went straight off to sleep – which is more than my poor CC did, as apparently the legs kept jerking at unexpected moments and woke him up.

It didn't happen every night, but often enough for my CC to start worrying. Then it started to happen in my arms and hands, so now if he wasn't being kicked to death he was being slapped across the face. I found out from other people with TM (see boring bit) that this is quite usual. However, it wasn't until I went to see my GP and happened to mention it, that I found out what it was called, and that there was a treatment for it.

Heigh ho.

MOBILITY (#2)

After my triumphant day on the shopping centre mobility scooter, I decide to go to the local supermarket. I deliberately pick a time when I hope it will be relatively empty and my CC manages to find a space in the "disabled" section of the car park, where I can triumphantly show my blue badge.

A word about the "blue badge" scheme. These days, this has replaced both the "orange badge" scheme, and the "registered as disabled" scheme, but a lot of people don't seem to realise this. When I was in hospital, they gave me a form so I could apply for the blue badge. According to this form, there was a list of Post Offices that would supply said badge, but I have to go "in person".

A couple of things are less than ideal about this. The first is that because my home is on the border between two counties (and hence two national health areas) the nearest Post Office on the list is about five miles away. The other thing is that I'm struggling round on two crutches and feel like death not-so warmed up.

I'm lucky in that my CC is home quite a bit, being retired, and is able to take me in his car. First problem over. Before we go out, I happen to mention I need a passport-sized photo, and I don't have one. My CC rings up the designated Post Office to ask if they have a photo booth. Just as well he's rung. They haven't.

This means that on the way, we have to drop in to the local post office, which has got one.

I struggle into the booth, and sit myself on the seat. On the wall in front of me, it suggests I might like to alter the chair height. No chance – I'm down, I stay down. CC gives me the required amount of money, then closes the curtain. I'm alone with a red light, a dull mirror and a list of instructions. I look in the mirror – not only do I feel like death-not-so-warmed-up, but I look like it as well. I don't care. I put the money in then stare straight ahead as the flash goes off four times.

Now comes the part where I have to get out of the booth and wait for my photos. I call my CC's name. No reply. With a bit of a struggle I manage to open the curtain and look out. I can't see him, he's gone.

There is nothing I can do. I can't even panic. He's taken my crutches with him so they won't fall over and damage someone, and there's nowhere for me to hold on to to pull myself up. Then I spot him over by the sweet counter. I call him in a sort of hiss. He doesn't hear. I try again, slightly louder. He still doesn't hear. He's got his back to me and he's forgotten to put in his hearing aid - again. I bellow. He hears me – so do all the other people waiting in the queue nearby. They all watch as he ambles over. "what's the matter? Are you done". I revert to hissing. "Yes. I can't get up." "What?" "I CAN'T GET UP" I bellow. I am the centre of attention as he leans over and grabs my arm so he can help me up. Then he picks up the now finished photos which slid out of the slot some time ago. "Oh dear" he says, "they don't look very good. Do you want another go?" I'm back to hissing. "No, let's go" and I grab my crutches and leave the room like a snail on speed.

We eventually get to the designated Post Office. There's nowhere to park. Immediately outside the PO there's two yellow lines and a bus stop. "You'll have to park here" I say. "But I can't" he says, "we haven't got a blue badge". I've had enough. All I want to do is go home, get into bed and pull the covers over me for the next year or so. "If you get done, I'll pay the fine" I say. "I can't walk from wherever we're going to be able to park, and anyway in about five minutes I'll *have* a blue badge." CC is not totally convinced, but he stops anyway.

We go in. I have to queue. I feel like falling over – never has a floor looked so appealing. I could just stretch out, go to sleep –

Next" bellows a voice. It's our turn. I go up to the counter. I suddenly realise I haven't got enough hands. Both my hands are busy holding me up on the crutches. But I need another hand to get the form and photos out of my handbag (strategically slung around my neck – a present from my mother when I realised I'd need a bag with a long strap). I give one crutch to my CC and, watched impatiently by the counter clerk I rummage in my bag for the relevant items. I hand them over, leaning on the edge of the counter and my remaining crutch. She does some jiggory pokery with various bits and pieces, then pushes something towards me. "Sign this" she barks. I'm now at a loss. If I let go of my crutch, I'll fall over. If I let go of the counter I will also fall over. I look at my CC. "You'll have to hold me up". He looks blank. "What?" I'm going to have to superglue his hearing aid in his ear, it's getting beyond a joke. The increasingly large queue behind us (surely they've got more than one counter clerk?) mutters in a slightly menacing way. I say again – louder – "you're going to have to hold me up". "Why?" (puzzled frown) "BECAUSE I'VE GOT TO SIGN THIS B****Y THING AND I'LL FALL OVER IF YOU DON'T". He gets the message – as do the queue and probably

34

anyone else passing the area within a hundred yard radius. He holds me up, I sign the paper, I get my Blue Badge.

As we leave, everyone gives us plenty of space. I am beginning to realise why disabled people can sometimes appear to be so aggressive. And I'm left wondering why it's essential for disabled people to get the blue badge in person, when it's so difficult because they're disabled. After all, if they weren't they wouldn't apply for a badge in the first place. Would they?

So to return to the story. We park in the disabled section of our local supermarket, and I put the blue badge on the dashboard. We've had to park a couple of spaces from the end of the bays because some bright spark put the two ATMs immediately next to the parking area, and the queue for money takes up the whole of the first bay. Very good planning on someone's part. Then we make another discovery. The doors in the supermarket that are immediately next to the end of the disabled parking bays are all fire doors and kept shut. The door we have to go through is about one hundred and fifty yards away. I can't walk that far. So my CC has to get the wheelchair out to push me into the shop.

We go up to the customer support counter, where a young man with acne flecked skin who looks about twelve is talking to a security guard. They pause to watch me approach. "I'd like to join the mobility scheme." He leans over the counter and looks down at me. "Pardon?" Oh no, not another one who needs a hearing aid. "The mobility scheme" I bellow, "how do I join?" He grins. His whole face is transformed. He's quite nice really – though he still looks about twelve. I need to sign a form and then next time I come in they'll have my card ready for me (it turned out this wasn't true – I still haven't got it) He then goes and gets one of the two electric buggies they possess. He needs to teach me how to use it. I struggle out of the chair and onto the buggy. It's fairly straightforward to use, logical really. Like everything else I've come across so far, it assumes full use of the hands. Still, I'll have a go.

Now there's a problem. My wheelchair. My CC says, "I'll put it back in the car" but I've already seen a sign on the buggy forbidding it's use outside the store. "I'll need it afterwards". The security guard says, "no probs love" and puts the chair out of the way behind the service desk. Nice man.

We set off. Now my CC doesn't shop the same way I do, even for food. My method is to cruise up and down each aisle in turn, thus reminding myself of everything I may need. He doesn't. I've yet to work out what his method is – it looks like random darting to me. Still, have buggy, will go by myself. This is the life.

I cruise up and down, stopping to let people move out of the way – I'm getting used to being ignored. It's better than running people over anyway. I can't see my CC, but I know what we'll need and I've got a *big* basket on the front. Excellent.

I'm quite enjoying myself. The only fly in my ointment of content is that I can't reach the higher shelves unless I get out of the buggy. This is ok, but makes me worry that if anyone sees me they might think I've got the buggy under false pretences. I mean, they don't know I can't walk very far, do they?

After about twenty happy minutes, I'm sitting in the wide "disabled access" queue with a bulging basket. There are about four people ahead of me when I realise there could be a problem How am I going to bag and carry the shopping. I call my CC on my mobile. "Where the h**l are you" he roars. "In the queue" He makes a sort of gobbling sound indicative of great stress. "You're WHERE" "In the checkout queue. And I'm going to need your help". A moment later he appears. "I don't like you on that thing" he snarls, "I can't see you and I don't know where you are."

Aha – independence at last!

He sorts out the shopping while I wait on the buggy. We put it all back in the buggy bag. As we approach the area where the buggy belongs, the helpful security guard approaches, wheeling my chair. "I'll put it away for you, love". A really really nice man. I get into my chair then my CC and I look at the bags of shopping. It looks a lot more than it did at the checkout. In the end, I wheel myself out to the car (gritting my teeth against the pain in my hands) with three bags perched precariously on my lap. Two bags are in the wheelchair shopping bag. My CC struggles along with the remaining five, trying to carry his car keys in his teeth.

And shopping used to be so easy!

BATHING BEAUTY

I have always thought that one of life's greatest luxuries (apart from a sleek white yacht, somewhere in the Mediterranean with handsome sailors and a glass of champagne in my hand - well I can imagine!) is wallowing in a sudsy, fragrant bath of hot water, surrounded by soft candlelight with a glass of something reasonably alcoholic and a good book. Before I got struck down, I had a very busy life, so I used to put "leisure time" in my diary, meaning "bath wallow" and I would always stick to it. It never occurred to me that there might come a time when bath time would be almost a nightmare.

Now our bathroom is extremely small. Not just small, but tiny. It's about six feet square, and to add to its lack of size is the fact that the ceiling is only at normal above-head height for eighteen inches before it starts rushing down at an angle, ending up at about three foot six over the taps end of the bath. The bit above the wash basin remains at normal height, which is how we can wash our hands without having to kneel on the floor.

The reason for this minute-ness is cast back in time. The house was originally built in the 30s as a council house, and as such it had three bedrooms, and an extension at the back on the ground floor containing the bathroom. (Some of the houses are still like that.) However, some bright spark decided to "modernise" the house sometime in the 60s or 70s, so they knocked down the extension and converted part of the largest bedroom as a bathroom.

So now the bedroom is much smaller, and the bathroom would suit mickey mouse.

I am having real problems with the bathroom. My CC – during his many years of sole occupation before I moved in – had fixed up a shower over the bath, at one side over the very narrow window. Being an engineer, he was able to fashion a rail which goes right round the bath and descends with the ceiling almost to tap height. This, however, means that an ordinary shower curtain won't fit, it has to be specially shaped. It's all very clever, but I'm now in the unenviable position of not being able to even have a shower without help.

When I was still in hospital, they wheeled me upstairs to a pretend bathroom in a room full of aids. Of course, at the time I had no idea of what I was going to need. In the hospital we had a shower with no cubicle, just a slight slope on the floor and a curtain round, together with a stool and handholds, which was relatively easy to use. It was a little unfortunate that this shower room was the only one accessible to the whole ward – men and women – but you learn to deal with it (usually with clenched teeth).

So back to the aids. The OT (short for Occupational Therapist – more of this later) asked if I had a shower over the bath at home. I said yes at which point she showed me a convenient plastic seat that fits over the bath, with handholds so you can get yourself on and off. I accepted the offer of having one, and it was at home by the time I left hospital.

Now this seat is probably a good idea in a conventional bathroom, but is causing problems in ours.

My CC carefully places it over the bath, makes sure it's safe and helps me onto it. So far, so good. Then we both realise that the special shower curtain can no longer do its job. The only solution is for my CC to draw it around me and help me to sit on it so the water will run down the curtain and end up back in the bath. This is not as easy as it seems, but after a bit of a struggle we manage it. The bottom of the curtain is weighted down with somethings that dig into my bum – although as most of the skin is completely insensitive this is not quite as bad as it sounds.

Now we both became aware of another problem. The shower head is in its holder a long way above my head, as are the shower controls, and I can't reach either.

Refusing to be stymied, we start again. My CC hands me the shower head before putting the curtain around (and under) me. But I still can't reach the shower controls. So he reaches round the curtain (just as well he's got long arms) pushes the button then whips his arm away, but not before the jet of water from the showerhead has soaked his shirt sleeve. (I was trying to hold the shower head away from myself until it reached the right temperature, and had inadvertently pointed it in his direction).

So far, having a shower has taken about quarter of an hour, and I still haven't washed.

The next difficulty becames obvious after I have (more or less successfully) hosed myself down. I need to use the shower foam which is in a push button pressurised container. I'd always thought it was inconvenient to only have two hands (though some of the guys I'd been out with in my far-distant youth seemed to have acquired more than the usual number) but now I realise I really *do* need another one. At least. Here I am, sitting on a plastic seat and part of the shower curtain with the shower head spraying water in one hand and a push button container in the other. And don't forget my hands don't work properly anyway.

In the end I solve the problem by holding the shower head between my knees which then leaves me free to use both hands on the shower foam container. It sort of works, but takes ages. By the time I've finished, and my CC has turned the shower off (this time with slightly less water down himself) I've spent over half an hour just having a shower, and am exhausted. My CC then suggests he wash my hair, so we pull the curtain back and he shampoos and conditions my hair within an inch of its life, while I sit shivering and feeling sick.

By the time he's got me dried off (I find I can't handle the towel by myself) and combed my hair, I have to go back to bed. I shall never think of showers as "quick" again.

So then we decide perhaps a bath would be easier.

Our bath is a smaller-than-usual one because of the lack of space, so I know I'm unlikely to slip down and drown. My CC having run the water and put in the bubbles, I try to get in.

The bath has handles on each side, but they're really not a lot of use. After some clumsy negotiation, we decide my CC should hang on to me for grim death while I lower myself in. Which works (after a fashion). So now I'm semi-recumbent in warm bubbly water, but it doesn't feel like luxury, and I have no desire for either alcohol or a good book. All my energy is aimed at trying to wash bits of me that I'd never viewed as inconvenient before (I leave this to your imagination) and wondering how I'm going to get out again.

There are two things to consider when getting out of the bath. One is how I'm actually going to get in an upright position without anything to hang onto, and the other, more immediate worry, is that the sloping roof above my head could cause a painful encounter if I try to stand up.

My CC however has no qualms about this at all. Under his instruction, I wriggle back in the bath, he then helps me get my feet under me, hangs onto my arm and hauls.

It feels extremely dangerous, and I am terrified I'm going to fall back into the bath (I don't know why I'm so bothered – the water will cushion my fall, and I can't feel much anyway. I suppose it's survival instinct). My CC is now talking to me through his teeth in a sort of semi-snarl. He obviously doesn't value my survival instinct as much as I do.

After a struggle I'm back on terra firma. My CC lowers me onto the closed lid of the loo so he can dry me. When he's finished, I'm exhausted (but dry) and he's exhausted (and wet) so we both go back to bed.

The remaining hurdle in this tiny water world is, of course, the loo. In the hospital, the two disabled persons loos had grab handles conveniently located nearby, and were slightly higher than normal, so I'd been lulled into a state of false confidence. However, the loo at home is a very different proposition. It is squashed between the bath and the wash basin, and there is a square beam next to it to hold the roof on. The beam's quite handy for siting the loo roll, but it can get in the way. The first time I tried to sit down, I realised there was little to hold on to, so now I do a sort of controlled drop, and hope I've aimed right. This works most of the time – though because the seat is so low, my CC sometimes has to help me get off again – this is the reason I carry my mobile into the bathroom with me if my CC is out, so I can phone (female) neighbours to come and rescue me.

This is where we once more enter the world of the OT.

OT OR NOT OT

I've been home over three months, and so far no-one has been to see me – healthcare professionals that is. Lots of other people have been, which is nice. Many of my visitors seem to be under the impression that, "once you're in the system they'll be throwing money and aids at you". Uh huh – I'm not convinced.

The telephone rings – it's an OT wanting to come and see me. Oh, joy. Maybe I can now stop using gravity and luck to get onto the loo.

She comes in due course – a nice lady. She asks how I'm coping. I'm not sure what to say really. I start talking about the bathroom. "May I look?" "Of course".

I tell her where it is – I've done one stair climb already today, and I can't manage another one just yet. As she starts to ascend, she notices the new rail. "I see you've got a rail" she says. Well, yes – they wouldn't let me out of hospital until I had one. "Yes", I say proudly, "My husband put it up when I was in hospital. Cost £80 from Focus". She frowns. "You shouldn't have had to pay for it" she says. *Now* they tell me. She goes upstairs while I wrestle with this one.

She comes back down. "That's impossible " she says. "No-one can put any aids in that". Oh, right. Thanks. Then she carries on, "luckily that's not my area". I look at her blankly. "I do settees and things". I continue to look blank. "To see if you need it up on blocks". My CC, having heard this last bit, comes in. "Oh, I can do that" he says, "couple of bits of wood should do it".

I am flapping at him. "What?" he says. "This lady" (I've already forgotten her name) "is going to do it. Properly", I hiss. "For free!"

"Ah" he says and subsides. Hallelujah, he's got his hearing aid in.

The OT checks which settee I use (we've got two) and promises to come back next day with the 'proper' blocks (whatever they are).

It's two days later. The OT came this morning and put a very complicated device under the feet of the settee. "Make sure they remain sited correctly" she says. "Especially after hoovering"

Right.

This afternoon I had a phone call from another OT asking to come and see me. Ah ha! This will be the one to put aids in the bathroom!

No.

When she arrives, she asks me how I'm managing. I tell her about the bathroom. She goes to look, pauses on the stairs. "I see you've got a hand rail. Good". I grunt.

She comes back down, shaking her head. "No way is there any room for adaptation. Very small. However, that's not my area". Right. "I'm here to look at your kitchen".

I think I'm getting the hang of this. There are obviously sub-categories of OT – so far I've had the settee one, and the kitchen one. Maybe the bathroom one will turn up soon.

We go into the kitchen. "Let's see if we can give you some help with the cooking" she says, looking round. Now I'm really impressed. I was a useless cook before I got ill – was I now going to become cordon bleu?

No. I realise that she was talking about adaptations. Shame. I get a rather funny look when she asks me whether I am okay with our existing saucepans and the level of the work tops and I reply, "haven't got a clue". Then she gets it – I obviously haven't been well enough to cook since I got home. "So do you manage to get proper meals?" My CC is standing silently in the doorway (only silent because if he opens his mouth the OT will see he is in fact curling up with laughter). "Of course" I say with dignity, "my husband does all the cooking". She looks around at this paragon of virtue. I mentally tell him not to say that he's *always* done the cooking because I'm so bad at it. Fortunately he's still trying to swallow his laughter, so he says nothing. As she's never met him before, I just hope that she thinks he always looks like that – sort of congested.

She then looks at the kettle – hurray, back in my territory – I'm getting quite good at coffee (decaffeinated of course). "We've got tippers" she says – well, there's no answer to that, is there. "Ah" I say, waiting for elucidation. "For the kettle" she goes on, "to help you pour out". She continues to look at the kettle. "However," she says, "we don't have a tipper big enough for this kettle". For a moment she broods about the fact that we don't fall in line with her model of an ideal, convertible kitchen, then her face brightens. "I know" she says, "you can buy a smaller kettle! One of those travel ones should do". I see. Mentally I think, "and I could just put less water in the kettle in the first place" but I don't want to ruin her pleasure at spending the money we haven't got.

She looks at me. "How are your hands?" Now what. "Not too good" I understate. "Well, you can get special knives and forks with bigger handles" she says. Oh, right. "If you can't find them in the shops, I can show you a catalogue". I'll bet you could, I think, but don't say. More money. No thank you, I'll continue to throw food all over the table.

Actually, it's turning into a sort of game. I haven't eaten at a restaurant since coming out of hospital – no energy, can't be bothered – so the only people to have seen my struggles are my CC and my parents, and we've turned it all into a bit of a joke. I'm okay as long as I keep to dry things – like peas, which don't stain the carpet as long as someone else picks them up.

"Now" – she's really getting into her stride now I'm beginning to conform. "What about a perching stool?" My mind is instantly filled with images of my grandfather's smallholding when I was a child. He kept hens. They perched. (I hated those hens. When I had to get the eggs I was in fear and trembling of their nasty beaks and beady little eyes. I would only go in once I was covered up like someone in the bomb squad). "Um" I say. "What's a perching stool?" I can't tell if she's pleased to be able to explain something, or getting annoyed with my obvious idiocy. "It's a stool with a slope" she says, "so you can perch" then, triumphantly "when you're preparing your meals".

I'm totally bemused. "Okay" I mutter.

"Good" she says, and prepares to move off.

As I trail behind her, out of the door (my CC has disappeared somewhere – he's probably out of earshot having hysterics) I suddenly remember something. The taps. Those horrible, small, swivelling monsters who sneer at me when I try to turn them on. "The taps" I say, brightly. She turns back to face me. "Ah!" she smiles, "are you having problems with them?". At last, she seems to be saying, something I can do. "I'm finding them practically impossible".

She looks at the taps. Her smile vanishes as if it's never been. "Are the taps upstairs the same as these?" she asks, meaningfully. "Well – yes". "Oh dear" she shakes her head. "I'm afraid they're completely the wrong sort for adaptation. You see, we've got handles we fit on. But they only go on the cross head taps". I'm amazed. "You mean those old fashioned things everyone used to have?" "That's right". "Of course" she continues, "you can always get the taps yourselves".

One week later, and I'm awaiting another OT. They're like buses – you don't see sight nor sign of one for months, then three come together.

This one's quite sweet, very tiny, and smiles a lot, which is nice. We sit down. I look down on her (my settee now being raised six inches above hers. It's been a talking point with visitors – I can really loom now). She tells me her name (which I instantly forget) and says, "I'm here to look at your bathroom".

At last! Frabjous day. This is the bathroom OT. My joy knows no bounds. Already in my imagination I'm having a long bath (did I mention the something alcoholic in my hand?) I'm sitting down gracefully on the loo (instead of doing a sort of reverse belly hop – if you see what I mean) and I'm having a shower without soaking my CC.

She recalls me to my surroundings. "I understand from my colleagues that it's a little – how shall I say – *difficult*".

"Well, apparently".

"Shall we go and have a look?"

She wants me to go as well, so I haul my bulk up the stairs – I'm still really using my arms to haul me up instead of my legs. It takes a while, but eventually we are standing outside the bathroom door.

It's a bit crowded – the landing's only really large enough for one-and-a-half. Good thing she's so tiny.

She goes in. I stand outside (no choice, the bathroom is only big enough for one). I lean against the wall and watch her, hoping she won't be too long.

She's turning slowly, looking rather thoughtful. My hope is coming to nothing – she's obviously up here for the duration. I say, "I'll see you back downstairs – I need to sit down" and I go down rather faster than I went up (Newton really knew his stuff – life is so much easier when gravity's on your side.)

Ten minutes later she comes down. There is something very disturbed in her eyes. My CC offers her a drink, and she accepts with relief. I don't think it's the need for caffeine (we haven't got any anyway) but having an excuse to wait longer to find the right words.

It doesn't work – she's obviously no nearer to sharing her findings when she's taken a sip. I decide to be kind. "Just tell it how it is, don't try to be tactful". She looks relieved.

"I'm afraid that this is just the worse bathroom for adaptations that I have ever seen." She takes another sip of coffee. Well, I can't complain – I did ask her to be honest. "Ah"

"Yes". She looks thoughtful. "I think we need to start looking at, maybe, an extension to the house". This one's even worse than the kitchen one – at least she only wanted us to buy kettles and taps. This one's in a different league altogether.

My CC is looking alarmed. "We can't afford anything like that." he says. She smiles. "There are grants available" she says. Then adds, "of course, in terms of disability you are very young". I like this OT – she can come again! "Yes" she continues, "as you get older you may start having problems with the stairs" she looks at me, thoughtfully, "and a stair lift just won't fit on your stairs, your legs are too long". Uh huh. There's no answer to this.

It turns out that she can do all the applying for us. We will be interviewed to see if we qualify for a council grant (it's means tested) or if we have to make a contribution. After that, a surveyor will come round and look at what needs doing. Then everything will be set in motion. Sounds good to me.

She does all the paperwork, and says, "you have to realise, though, that you will get what you need and not necessarily what you want." Sounds ominous. She then adds, "I'll put you down as an emergency as you're struggling. It means you won't have to wait quite so long". As she gets to the front door on her way out, my CC says, "how long do you think it will take?" She looks thoughtful, then says, "the interview for the grant should happen in about six to nine months time". Then she leaves.

My CC and I are left looking at each other in dismay. I am thinking how long nine months felt when I was pregnant – and I have the feeling it's going to feel a lot longer this time!

POND PARTY

I am a very keen gardener, and as the spring comes I begin to get rather frustrated at my lack of physical movement. I'm dying to get out there, pulling up weeds and trimming things. However, the biggest frustration is the pond.

When I first arrived in this house, my CC showed little apparent interest in the garden. It's quite big, with a long garden shed to one side and another shed at the bottom. One side is straight and the other at an angle, so the bottom of the garden is narrower than the top. My CC had thought of it as a dog toilet, but as he no longer has a dog, I think a change of use is in order – say, to a garden. I've done quite a bit, and it's starting to look nice.

Now I've always loved water (though not to drink – see D E eight) – I think there is nothing lovelier than sitting outside in the nice weather, sipping a glass of something appropriate and listening to the sound of running water. My CC took a bit of persuading when I first said I'd like to put in a water feature. His immediate response was to say, "I'll stand in the garden; you keep me topped up with lager and give me a bucket, then I'll give you a water feature". Needless to say, I ignored this offer, and went ahead with the feature.

The first thing I put in was a five-sided wooden pond – quite small with a little fountain. I half buried it in the grass next to the patio, and gradually my CC got used to it. Then last year I started work on a pond, using the same part of the garden. Some of the digging was already done, all I had to do was take out the existing water feature then dig some more.

Now in my previous garden (pre-CC) I had built a wildlife pond with a butyl liner, lots of ledges and rocks all round through which flowed a little stream which cascaded down into the pond. Though I say it myself, it was rather good, and even better when it started acquiring some life of its own – frogs, various insects and other delightful things. So I decided to repeat my success in the new garden.

I hit a snag fairly early on – my last garden had been on a slope, running down towards the house, so the stream and waterfall had been fairly straightforward. This new garden, however, does not have a similar topography, so I had to do some quick thinking. I decided to go for a more formal shape, and happily set off with a spade, digging my hole, adding butyl lining and filling it up with water.

Now I won't say it was a complete disaster, nothing I couldn't sort out (as I thought) so I was content to leave it until this spring in the knowledge that I need only take a couple of days to do it.

Of course the awful truth is that now the spring is here and I'm unable to do anything. I look at our bank balance, and realise I can't even afford to book anyone to come and do it for me.

I'm sitting having a moan at my friend, S, when she suddenly says, "why don't you have a pond party?"

"A what?"

"A pond party. You supply the food and drink" (I knew drink would come into it somewhere!) "ask all your friends to come and help, make a plan of what you want, and there you are".

Now as ideas go, this has to be one of the best I've ever heard. So without further ado, I ring up virtually everyone I know and start the ball rolling.

On the day I exhaust myself setting out the table with dippy things and cheesy things and all sorts of other things. There are not very many people coming after all, what with holidays and teaching schedules and so forth, but there will be enough to accomplish Plan Pond. The men have been volunteered by their
wives to do the actual digging, the rest of us are going to sit around, having drinks, watching the men work and occasionally shouting encouraging remarks. I'm looking forward to this.

The first couple of people arrive, so CC makes coffee while we look out of the window. At almost the exact moment, black clouds begin to loom ominously. "It might pass over" I say, hopefully.

As a couple more people come in, the sky gets even blacker. I am still hopeful.

Ten minutes later, as the last four arrive, the heavens open.

Now in preparation for today, my CC has emptied the pond, and put the five fish and plant ponds in a tank. All that needs doing now is for the liner to be taken out and washed down, the hole enlarged and straightened, then the liner to go back and be filled up with water. Then it's going to have a row of slabs all round and voila, a pond.

Gloomily I look out of the kitchen window as one of the heaviest outbursts of rain I have ever seen outside the

European mainland lashes at the garden, and begins to fill up the pond again.

We all stand around, and wonder what to do. My CC has a word with one of his sons, and the pair of them bravely venture out. The rest of us start opening bottles, and watch in admiration as the two of them, almost ghost-like in the torrential rain, pull the liner out of the pond, and hose it down. They come in to general acclaim, shaking water off themselves like a couple of huge dogs.

I'm still a little hopeful, but to tell the truth I begin to realise we're probably going to have the party but not the pond. I put some background music on, and we all help ourselves to food and drink.

As far as parties go, this one is hugely successful. Everyone has a lovely chat, whilst demolishing the pile of food on the table. Our house feels very full, as there are too many people to fit in the front room, so it overflows into the kitchen, but no-one seems to mind.

Eventually the last people leave at about nine at night. The rain has not let up for an instant. I go to bed, exhausted.

It's two days later. I've been in tears continuously because I now have a big muddy hole in the garden full of water, instead of a proper pond. Today, of course, it's dry. It would be – there's no-one around to do the work. My CC has offered to do it for me, but he's got a bad back, and I don't think it would be fair to ask him – he does enough for me already.

Suddenly, the doorbell goes. It's my friend, S, the one who originally made the pond party suggestion. Her husband comes in behind her, carrying a large spade. "We've come to do your pond" they say, "so let's get cracking".

My friend's husband and my CC dig for six hours. They square-up the hole, making it bigger and deeper, then put a shelf all round to take the slabs. They use spirit levels to make sure it's all straight, and by the end of the day I have a new pond, liner in, awaiting slabs, which my CC will cement in the next day.

There are so many things to be grateful for, even when a lot of your daily activities have been unexpectedly curtailed or made extremely difficult, but top of my list are friends and family who don't mind putting themselves out so that they can help to make you smile!

MOBILITY #THREE

I have decided that what I really need is a scooter. Not the phut phut 49cc type (I used to have one of those – most unpleasant in the snow) but what is termed a "mobility scooter". I've seen people sailing around serenely and it looks really easy. It would mean that my CC can go back to work (part time) and I won't be stranded. I imagine myself, all flowing skirts and floral tops, pottering around the village shops enjoying the independence. I've got a bit of money – back pay from my DLA – and it seems an appropriate use.

As a starting point, I go onto the internet (always my first port of call these days) and Google "mobility scooters" (for those of you still in the steam age, Google is the most popular computer search engine around – you put your word or words in, then wait to see what it brings up).

I get onto a big site immediately, and start to look at pictures of scooters. Ten minutes later, I'm feeling depressed. I knew that new scooters were going to be way out of my reach, but £1500! I could get a car with that! (if I had it, of course. Which I don't. Because I can't work 'cos I'm off sick. Which is why I need a scooter. Ever heard a better illustration of chicken-and-egg?) So I start looking at second hand scooters. There are so many – I'm bewildered. I decide I need to talk to an expert. I contact the firm by e-mail, and they ring me the same day.

In due course, I open the door to a young, nicely turned out man who informs me he's come down all the way from Leeds! Not especially for me of course, but because one of his sales team is off sick. *His* sales team? He looks barely old enough to be out of school uniform.

I make him a cup of tea, and he carries it through to the front room for me. Nice manners. We settle down for a discussion on my "needs". He shows me a few pictures, and explains all the different types of scooter. I specifically want one to fit into the boot of the car, so my CC and I can go out together sometimes. I'm fairly sure in my own mind that these lightweight scooters are cheaper than their larger cousins.

Wrong!

I've already told him I can't afford a new one, but a second hand one might be feasible. He leans forward, putting the catalogue down. "Could I ask you what your budget is, please?" He's asked nicely, so I tell him.

"£250.00"

To do him credit, he doesn't laugh. He doesn't say, "you're wasting my time". He doesn't get up and walk out. Instead he explains, very carefully, that if I want a second hand scooter from his company, it will cost a minimum of £450.00! I try not to gape at him. I'm beginning to see my dream go up in smoke.

I think he probably understands my reaction, and, being the nice young man he is, he starts to suggest other places I could look ("local paper, e-bay"). He then gives me his card, and says anytime I find what I'm looking for, if I have any queries to ring him and he'll tell me if it's any good or not. As I wave him off, I think what a good salesman he is. He seemed to be genuinely caring and helpful, going out of his way to assist. Of course, it now means I will recommend his firm to whoever asks, maybe that's the idea. Either way, he's left me feeling there are other avenues to explore.

I discuss it with my CC. I often buy thing from e-bay (for those of you who've been living down a hole it's a big online auction site) so I've got the general idea of how it works. I had a sudden ghastly thought, "it'll cost a bomb in postage". My CC smiles, tolerantly. "We'll go and get it if you find one. Just make sure it's within a hundred miles".

I'm onto e-bay without further ado. My goodness, the number of scooters is quite staggering. The nice young man from the scooter company has already told me there's quite a few sloshing about because people "cease to need them" and the next of kin want to get rid of them. Hmmm!

I look down the list – I'm bewildered. So I reconfigure to show me from cheapest to dearest – much better. Amidst all the "buy now, £500" and, "bids now standing at £550" I spot one without a lower price. Aha! It's a lightweight, transportable scooter which will easily fold up and go in the boot of any average car. I take the name and model ("Wispa") and look at the big site for scooters. It's there. I read the description. It seems to be exactly what I want.

I go back to e-bay and look at the seller rating – 100%. Can't get better than that. (Seller rating is a useful way to see if the seller is genuine, in which case he gets positive feedback, or not good at delivering or revealing faults, something like that, in which case his rating goes down accordingly. I only know all this because my children have told me). With a feeling akin to excitement, I bid my maximum of £250.00. Then I do what I always do, and go away and do something else until after the auction closing time. I'd noticed that there were other bids on the scooter, so I'm not wildly optimistic. Still it's a start. And the owner of the scooter lives about fifteen miles away, which is useful.

Well, I think I'm meant to have this scooter. When I check the site after the bidding's finished, I find I've won – for £180.00! I've got £70 left over! Hurrah!
As requested, I phone the owner to arrange pick up, and we decide my CC and I will go over the following afternoon.

I don't get much sleep that night. I alternate between delight at actually getting a scooter so cheaply and dismay at the thought there might be something drastically wrong with it that the owner's not saying.

The next afternoon finds us outside – the wrong house, as it turns out. Good start. I'd missed seeing the "A" after the house number. I mumble an apology to the woman who'd opens the door, but she seems ok about it. In turns out that the seller is her father and he lives next door!
We finally find ourselves in the – right – house, gazing at a lovely little neat dark blue scooter. It is love at first sight. There is a genuine reason for selling, so that's alright. The owner shows my CC how it comes apart, and how to charge up the batteries. I already know that it does fifteen miles to the battery (on the flat) with a top speed of four miles an hour. Wouldn't suit Brands Hatch, but it'll do for me.

The owner asks me if I'd like to try it out, but I really don't want to make my (possibly wobbly) debut in front of a stranger, however nice, so I decline, my CC puts it in the car, I pay the nice man the cash and away we go.

Next day, the battery is nicely charged up, I've downloaded an instruction book from the internet (what would I do without it!) and I'm ready for my first sojourn. How eager I am, as I sit on the little black seat. It's even got arms! I'm confident I'll be alright – after all, I've used scooters before.

Oh, boy! The scooters I've used previously have been sturdy, heavy duty jobs, and I only used them around the shops on flat surfaces. How very different everything is now!

My CC is walking behind me (again) watching me. The first thing he says, as I prepare to set off, is, "Tuck your skirt in, otherwise you'll get it wrapped around the wheel". There goes part of my picture. No flowing robes, then. The best way I can think of to tuck in my skirt is wrapping it around and between my legs, which is a bit tricky (not helped by my CC's helpful suggestion of, "just tuck it into your knickers". And they say gallantry is dead!) Eventually he's satisfied that I'm not going to do an Isadora Duncan, and we set off.

I don't know if you've ever thought about it – I certainly hadn't – but pavements tend not to be flat and level. Pavements outside houses slope gradually down to the road, so the cars can get out of their drives easily. It might make it easy in a car, but you should try it on a small mobility scooter. Suddenly I'm on one of these slopes, and my scooter begins to lean sideways. I'm terrified it's going to fall over, and try to adjust. I over-compensate, and find myself hurtling towards the road (I know I'm only doing four miles man hour, but it *feels* like hurtling). My CC is shouting something – what is it? An eternity passes, during which I could have read War and Peace, before I realise what he's saying. "Stop! Stop!" I take my thumb off the forward control (right thumb for forward, left thumb for reverse) and the scooter stops. Immediately. I feel like a rider whose horse has refused a fence. I slide sideways and forward, my handbag falls out of the basket in front, I'm half lying on the road and my CC has to come and help me up.

I sling my handbag round my body, get back on the scooter (which my CC has steered away from the road) and prepare to proceed (at a much slower pace). Before I move, my CC snaps, "skirt". I mutter to myself as I wrap the skirt around myself again. We set off.

When we get to the main road, I suddenly realise that I can't just cross it like I used to. The scooter can't handle heights of more than a couple of inches, if that, and the kerb is a good six inches high. I have to look for a spot where the pavement slopes down to give me access to the road – and I have to check there's a matching slope on the other side of the road. I'm glad I've got my CC with me, otherwise I know I'd chicken out and go home – if I could work out how to turn the scooter round, that is.

Having negotiated the road crossing, I sail into the park, and relax a bit. There's a broad, smooth tarmac path leading straight down into the village, and I feel confident I can handle it.

Do you know how many lumps, bumps and little slopes there are in a smooth looking public path? I'll tell you – too many. Before long I realise that using the scooter will have an added bonus – a full body workout as I lean this way and that to counteract the effect of the pavement on the scooter!

MOBILITY #FOUR

I'm reasonably confident on my scooter now. I've been into the village a few times, and my CC has put a couple of hooks on the back of the seat to hold my stick (I've graduated to one stick and got rid of the crutches – ah bliss!) I've sussed-out all the crossing points in the village, and realised (after the first shopping trip) that the basket is miniscule, and hanging carrier bags on the handle slows the scooter down (I think it was probably the weight of the box of wine, but we all need to make sacrifices). So I have to work out my route very carefully. It takes quite a few trips before I'm confident enough to cross the high street, but at least the co-op's on my side of the road.

The day has come when I'm going to try my scooter out on the streets of a foreign land – well, Wales. We're due at Brecon as my CC is involved in the jazz festival, and we're going to stay with D & C (whoops – I'd better reverse that!) C & D, our kind friends, who understand what has happened to me.

When we arrive outside their house, I suddenly realise how steep the pavement is into the town. Even if I risked going *down* the hill, I'll never get back up.

We mull this over whilst sipping red wine (I told you they were nice!) and came to the conclusion we'd leave the scooter parked safely in the RAF club in town (where C is heavily involved, and where CC's marching band is based.)

So this is what we do.

I still find I get fatigued fairly quickly (it's not just feeling deadly tired, but I feel sick as well) but C is always there with a cup of tea, a helping hand or the offer of the bed to sleep in whenever I need it.

On our last full day, Sunday, C takes me to the RAF club in the car. I've been taking part in the jazz service in the Cathedral, and feel quite good. I had thought I'd be tired, but I now find myself wide awake. So we follow the band down the hill, and C drops me off by the club.

I decide I'm going to take the bull by the horns, and go round the town on my own. Previously either C or a member of her family has walked with me, making sure I was safe, but I feel the time has come to strike out on my own (perhaps not the happiest of allegories, but it'll have to do).

I ride out of the club, feeling happy, The weather is lovely (for a change) not too hot, but plenty of sunshine. The streets in the centre of town have been closed to traffic for the duration of the festival, and people are everywhere, spilling into the roads when there is not enough room on the pavements.

I'm proud of myself – I'd thought ahead, and started in the road, so I have no pavements to contend with. I go round the corner and suddenly feel as if I'm on an old "bone shaker". The road has cobbles – looks nice, murder to ride on. However, I negotiate it successfully, and trundle happily towards my favourite shops.

Suddenly I feel as if a giant hand has grabbed me. It's most peculiar – I'm being pulled – hard – by my right leg. And almost instantly I know what has happened. I stop the scooter, then look mournfully down and behind me. What my CC has predicted has come true — my favourite gorgeous gypsy skirt has wrapped itself around the back wheel and is hugging it closely with no sign of letting go. I ponder for a moment or two, then decide the best thing to do is go backwards (left thumb) whilst carefully pulling my skirt (right hand). With a bit of luck I haven't done any damage and my CC need never know. As I begin to perform this manoeuvre, a voice way above my head says, "are you alright? Do you need some help?" Of course, if this was a film the speaker would be tall, dark haired, blue eyes with an amazing figure — but this is real life, so standing there was an elderly tall, thin man with a kindly smile. I can feel myself going hot, then cold, with embarrassment. Just for a second I contemplate fainting a la heroines of old — but there were no scooters in those scenarios, and anyway it wouldn't help to rescue my skirt.

I am hassled — I will admit — and give my precious skirt a bit of a yank so I can just get out of there. There is an ominous tearing sound, and suddenly I find myself sitting surrounded by torn skirt. I look at my erstwhile helper glumly. "He's going to kill me. He's always telling me to tuck my skirt in. And this is my favourite skirt". The elderly man, though kindly, obviously suspects me of some kind of lunacy — or maybe he doesn't like the thought of an aggressive "he" and he says, "so long as you're alright then." "I'm fine" I lie, "Thank you so much for your concern" thus giving him a good exit line.

I feel distraught. My favourite skirt — I'll never be able to wear it again. And I've got to go through the streets of Brecon looking like a ragamuffin. I gather my skirt around me and, showing rather more leg than I would normally feel inclined to, I set off back to the club. Gone are my ideas of looking in the charity shop, and the shoe shop, and the ....

never mind, you get the picture. The only good thing is I can't hear the band yet, so with a bit of luck I'll be able to get myself ensconced in a seat in the club with the tear in my skirt (hopefully) disguised enough for me to choose my moment when telling my CC he was right.

In my preoccupation, I don't realise I'm heading back on the pavement – until I suddenly see a barrier across the pavement just in front of me. I stop and weigh up my options. I could back up – there's no room to turn round without risking an eighteen-inch drop onto the road. Not good. I could sit there all day and wait to be rescued. Not an option. So I do the only thing I can. I get off the scooter, holding my skirt with my left hand and grab my stick with my right. I then approach two men standing drinking and having a chat.

Now I would normally not approach strange men for any reason however dire, but this is the jazz festival, and these two looked like typical jazzers. I take the chance. "Excuse me," I hear myself saying, "is there a nice, strong man here who can put my scooter on the road please". Oh no, now it's "Gone with the wind" time. I'm probably simpering as well. Then one of the men smiles, hands his drink to the other (a very trusting move, I feel) and, saying "of course" swings my scooter off the pavement and into the road as if it was a feather.

I scoot off, waving merrily (whilst clutching my skirt) and feeling much cheered, mentally rehearsing how I'm going to tell my CC about my catastrophe. I am reconciled to the certain knowledge that he is going to feel smug for at least a week.

IN MY DREAMS I'M DANCING

My CC has a wonderful ability. He says that when he's dreaming, if it turns into a nightmare he can order himself to wake up. That's all very well if you *know* you're dreaming. I never know. My dreams are always vivid and real and I am totally absorbed by them.

So here I am at our favourite jazz club. I can't remember who the band are, but they're very hot and swinging. My CC and I are on the dance floor, jiving and having fun. He's spinning me on the spot and as I spin I can see the other dancers around us as I whiz by. I'm elegant and light as a feather. I look up at my CC and he's smiling at me.

Now the band change the rhythm – it's a quick step. My CC and I are the only dancers on the floor as we swoop and glide, effortlessly turning corners and achieving complicated moves. I feel wonderful. My body is working perfectly, there is no pain, no numbness, I am alive and happy. I relish the attention from the rest of the jazz-goers as they applaud in mute admiration at our prowess.

When I wake up, I think I've gone to sleep and am having a nightmare. I try to do what my CC does, and tell myself to wake up.

It's not possible. I'm actually awake. Reality crashes in on me.

For a while I lie still, trying to recapture the magic of my dream before it disappears. but however hard I try, it begins to shred and fade like gossamer on the wind.

I think this is probably the hardest moment of my day. The one when reality hits me again and I know I face another twelve hours of pain and struggle. I can only allow myself to wallow in self-pity for a short time, otherwise I know I'll never get up.

I have developed a method for getting out of bed – thank goodness for small rooms! I manoeuvre myself until I am sitting on the edge of the bed with my feet on the floor, then one-two-three – I push myself up and catch my weight with my hands flat against the wall. If I stagger, I just sit back on the bed and try again. It's a method that serves me well. My aim is to get around without falling over – once down, I can't get up again without help. Which come to think of it, gives me a lot in common with tortoises.

I wonder if tortoises dream?...............

ANNIVERSARY

Here I am, one year from when I became ill. A lot has happened in that year – and most of it recently! I'm sitting on the sofa in the front room, before a blazing "mock" coal fire with a glass of champagne in my hand, toasting the progress we have made together, my CC and I. Life is always an adventure, and as with most adventures, is more exciting when looking forward than looking back.

I have a lot to be grateful for. My CC (who is going to have a lesson in hair management after my hairdresser recently had to cut an inch-and-a-half off the ends because of damage – will someone please explain nicely to male carers like mine that conditioner is not rubbed in hectically like shampoo!!!), my kids, my brother and my parents, who have all supported in their various ways and kept me sane; my friends – some old, some new (in terms of friendship age not physical age!) who still treat me like a human being, my fabulous GP who gives up his time for me and is ever thoughtful (what other doctor would notice your appointment is at 9.00am and, knowing you can't really "do" mornings, changes your appointment to later in the day);the TM support group (may they continue to grow!); Jonathan who is helping me through this maze with the light of reason. As I look out through the darkened window, I can see the first snow of the year silently spiralling down through the uncurtained light, and I think of all the things I have in my life that I have time to appreciate. And now I have a new specialist, who will take me through exactly what has happened, a one-to-one physio who devises special exercises just for me and the lovely Dee, who helps me on the toning tables twice a week.

So I raise my glass in a silent toast – thank you everyone who is helping to make my life such fun. And to you, dear Reader, for sharing this crazy journey with me. I hope it has given some insights along the way into a world that I wish you will never have to enter.

Cheers!!!

TRANSVERSE MYELITIS

A PERSONAL VIEW

DOESN'T IT MEAN TRADEMARK?

So what is it you've got? T M? Doesn't that stand for trademark?

I knew I was ill. I was in Liverpool, a long way from my home south-west of Birmingham, and I was working with a group of very talented girls preparing a Music Theatre spot for a performance in a couple of days' time. I couldn't remember a time when I felt so tired, and using the energy that I needed to draw the best out of the girls, whilst teaching them the skills they would need, was turning me into a wreck.

Each night I would go back to my hotel in the docks, have an early dinner at a small table looking out over the water, and feel so tired that as soon as my pudding was finished I would go to my room and crash out.

Each day got worse, and the night of the performance seemed to go on forever. I had to wait for the taxi to take me back my hotel immediately after the show. The others were staying to party, but I knew I'd had enough.

I arrived home the next day after two train journeys, with three hours to spare before I had to start teaching again, and I thought, wow that bed looks inviting! I was in, I was asleep, the alarm went off and I knew there was no way I was getting out of this bed again for a while at least. My mobile was next to me - I used it. Then I slept, and slept, and slept.

Most viruses, even unpleasant ones like this, have their day, party through your system, then get kicked out by your immune system and go and find someone else to annoy. They do not usually let you wake up one morning and find that half of your lower body is paralysed.

I dragged myself to the doctor's surgery. She said, " give it a week. If it's still not right come a back and we'll have a closer look."

One week later I re-presented myself. there was no change, the whole of my left lower half was numb. this time she suggested it was sciatica, and I was left to find my own way to the local hospital for an X-ray. And another week's wait. I phoned in. The X-ray was clear. I asked for another sick note. And another doctor's appointment.

This time, I saw a different doctor in the same practice and went through the same tired routine. This time was different. He asked me to wait until he'd seen his last two patients, then come back - and in the meantime to ask my husband to come down. We went back in. He phoned up the neuro department at the Queen Elizabeth Hospital in Birmingham, gave them the symptoms, and my mobile phone number, hung up and asked me to be ready to be admitted to hospital.

One hour later they phoned me. That same day I was ensconced in a clean sheeted uncomfortable hospital bed in one of neuro wards.

For three weeks I was tested, filled up with steroids, moved around in my bed to different parts of the (mixed sex) ward and visited by various white-coated individuals of differing ages and experiences. I discovered that I could only have an MRI scan when knocked out by sedatives - I knew I was claustrophobic, but it never really given it a test like this!

Eventually, the specialist from on high deigned to visit my hospital bed. There was a diagnosis. It was transverse myelitis. Otherwise known as TM. I'd never heard of it. Doesn't it mean Trade Mark?

* *

Knowing what is wrong with you is not always the end of the story. Sometimes, it's not even the beginning. When the specialist told me what was wrong, and even when his sidekick came back to have a long talk with me about what could be ahead, I still had no idea what was awaiting me. There was no question of going back to work for some months - it would be reviewed. There was no way of knowing how long it would take me to be able to walk properly again. I would have episodes of extreme fatigue, when I would be unable to do anything but sleep. None of this information seemed to sink in. I remained cheerful, positive, smiling and chatting to my visitors. No one seemed able to understand my attitude, they were all in pieces around me. They didn't understand me, and I didn't understand them.

There was physio every day except weekends of course. And I slowly began to get an inkling of what my future was going to be like. The simplest movements - which were too simple for me to even attempted before – were now out of my reach. " lift your leg slowly" they said. I tried, I really tried. Sweat was pouring off me. and I kept trying. I felt sick. and I kept trying. Eventually, I could lift my leg. At which point, they gave me other exercises. my left leg was weak, and now they found so was my right arm. I kept trying.

Just before I left hospital, I saw the Occupational Therapist. We went to the mock bathroom, to look at adaptations and aids. I had absolutely no idea what I was going to need at home. I guessed. I was told I was going to need an extra rail to get up the stairs, I couldn't be allowed home until it was in place and my husband paid up and put one in. Only later did we find out we didn't need to pay for it ourselves. No-one came to our home to look.

I got home just before Christmas. There was no time for buying presents, I had sent some cards from hospital, and that would have to do. My husband came home from the shops with a miniature fibre optic Christmas-tree which we put on the sideboard.

Time passed. I found out all the things I could no longer do. But I stayed cheerful. This would soon pass, or I would find a way round it. The fatigue which hit out of the blue was a nuisance, admittedly, but that too would pass. I went to my son's wedding in a castle in Scotland, and we adapted our journey so we took two days going up, shortened our stay, and took two days getting back. Now I could look forward to handling my disability, sleeping off the fatigue and getting back to work.

Then it all changed. I woke up one day, and the numbness had spread to my arms and hands. At first my hands were so sensitive that I was unable to touch anything without feeling intense pain. Then, slowly, over the course of a week, the feeling began to go out of my hands. Now reality hit. I could do very little. I could dress myself - slowly - but had to restrict myself to clothes that would pull on without buttons. All my lovely shoes were put aside in favour of slip-ons. I could neither bath nor shower without help. By now, my parents had bought me a wheelchair. There were days when I just wanted to cry and cry - and there were other days when I did just that. My frustration was incredible.

I tried to stay cheerful when I saw or spoke to friends and relatives. They called me heroic, a saint. They said they didn't know how I did it. I said they didn't see me when they weren't there. They said, " What it is it you've got?" I said," TM". They said," doesn't that mean Trade Mark?"

* * * * * * * * * * * * * * * * *

Self-pity can feel a very safe state - sometimes you don't even recognise it for what it is. You can wallow like a pig in muck. and it can last for very long time. You bring other people down with you, and because you are disabled and ill, they let you do it.

I went there for a while. But not for long. I started wanting to know. I researched TM on the web, I joined the TM association based in America, I got leaflets to tell my friends what the problem was and how to deal with it. I explained it was an auto-immune response, probably triggered by my virus, which had caused inflammation in my spine, and damage to the nerves.

Because I was a touch typist, and could no longer use my keyboard properly, I bought a copy of ViaVoice. Although frustrating in its own way, heading off into its own little realms of text which bore no reality to what I had just said, I found it's little side trips amusing and realised that even with the corrections it was still faster than doing it myself, so I persevered.

There were still times of huge frustration, not helped by the lack of information as to what was available to me, the length of time it took for any assessment or action to help me, the lack of communication between different NHS Departments and areas and the feeling that I had just been dumped.

I had long talks with my GP - the one who had picked up on my TM. It turned out that he'd seen it before in hospital. The average GP could go for one hundred years without ever seeing a case, it's so rare. He tells it like it is. If he doesn't know, he says so. He told me that the most important thing in my life now was my support network. I realised that unlike many people, I was blessed with husband, family, and friends who cared and wanted to help me.

I'm waiting for him to receive the results of my second MRI scan. It has been several weeks since the scan was taken, but due to inefficiencies in the system, copies have not yet been sent to him. As soon as he has had a chance to see them, he has assured me he will visit and explain the findings.

In the meantime, I am slowly adapting to what could be my permanent state. I am slowly building up my strength, and day on day I am able to do more and more. I still need to use the wheelchair if I have to go any distance, but I am now used to shopping at other people's crotch level, gazing small children in pushchairs in the eyes. I have received a key issued by radar which will enable me to use every disabled toilet the country - although like everything else I have experienced in the last few months, it was a while before I found out about this facility.

One of the things I have been told is that I must avoid stress. I sometimes think this is going to be my biggest challenge. Some days it's as if I was being deliberately tested! From inefficiency in a certain government department, which nearly led to unnecessary court action, to the washing-machine breaking down and having to be replaced, I could be tearing my hair out. However, as I've been told that I need to regularly do my breathing exercises, as my diaphragm is not working properly, I kill two birds with one stone. Diaphragm strengthening leads to stress busting!

The future is very uncertain. But the most important thing is that this illness is not life-threatening. The uncertainties are to do with my day-to-day activities, when I can get back to work, and how much I will be able to do when I get there. I have not ruled out the possibility of retraining in some area. I have been offered opportunities for training within my present employment, and this all leads to positive feelings.

Whatever happens, I now feel that I understand this new world in a better way than I did before. The world of the so-called "disabled" is one which able- bodied people, no matter how willing, can never imagine in its entirety. There is a lot to be said for disabled people having maximum input into facilities which are designed for their use. The day-to-day living can become extremely difficult, and is not helped by even small things like a lack of access to favourite shops and places of entertainment. Although action is being taken in those directions, there is still so much to be done. The lack of awareness in the general public is quite extraordinary. Until it happens to you, you move around in your own world oblivious to the difficulties of others to move within that same world with you. Perhaps everyone should be made to use wheelchairs for a day to see how it feels.

I began this piece almost as a diary. I finished it sounding more like a campaigner. Perhaps there is a lesson for me here. In the meantime, I shall continue taking things as they come, resting when I need to, going out when I can, and really enjoying those things that previously I took for granted - all those who love me and who I love - and the fact that I am still here to annoy people!

TRANSVERSE MYELITIS

THE FACTS

(THE BORING BIT!)

TRANSVERSE MYELITIS
(excerpts reproduced from TM Society leaflets with permission)

Transverse Myelitis is not very common in the UK. It is estimated there are only about 300 new cases a year. This means that on average it will take 100 years before every GP encounters one person with the condition.

WHAT IS TM? (1)

TM is a rare neurological disorder, one of a group of "neuroimmunologic" diseases of the central nervous system. There is tremendous variability in the presentation of symptoms, which are based on the level of the spinal cord affected and on the severity of the damage to the myelin and the neurons in the spinal cord. The symptoms of TM include muscle weakness, paralysis. parasthesias or uncomfortable nerve sensations, neuropathic pain, spasticity, fatigue, depression and bladder, bowel and sexual dysfunction.

TM can be acute or slow developing. There are several variations of TM diagnosis as well.

CAUSES OF TM

TM may occur in isolation or with another illness. When TM occurs without apparent underlying cause,. it is referred to as idiopathic. Idiopathic TM is assumed to be a result of abnormal activation of the immune system against the spinal cord. TM often develops alongside viral and bacterial infections.

Approximately one-third of patients with TM report a flu-like illness with fever, around the time of the onset of neurological symptoms.

WHAT IS TIM? (2)

TM is a rare disorder, involving an inflammatory attack in the central nervous system. This could happen anywhere along the spinal cord, causing a "lesion" usually visible on an MRI scan.

Attacks are normally one-off episodes, but sometimes recur in different places along the spinal cord. Some people severely affected initially can go on to make a good recovery over the first 6 months following an attack. Most are permanently affected to some degree.

At the point of attack, the outer sheath of the nerves is damaged, causing a disturbance in the signals sent along the nerve to the corresponding muscles. Imagine an electrical lead that has lost part of its insulating plastic cover. The appliance attached to this lead is likely to "short circuit" and be unreliable. The same is true for muscles which are controlled by the damaged nerves.

The type of nerve damage is known as "demyelination" and TM is a "demyelinating disease" in the same family of conditions as Multiple Sclerosis.

People are affected by TM in different ways and with different degrees of severity. It is important to remember that just because you can't see what is wrong, it doesn't mean the TM sufferer is not feeling pain or discomfort. They may find it difficult to explain exactly how they feel.

You may also notice that people with TM have "good" days and "bad" days. Over time we can learn what triggers the bad days.

Typically stress, overdoing things and getting hot and bothered can worsen symptoms, or contracting another illness.

Symptoms are often felt in the legs and feet, and/or the arms, hands and chest, depending on the position of the lesion.

One of the most common symptoms is extreme tiredness or fatigue.

The muscles affected by TM will tire quickly and also be prone to spasm, which is like a sharp cramp that can last for days. Sometimes the limbs affected can twitch, which may look a bit strange if you're not used to it.

Almost everyone with TM suffers some degree of difficulty with walking. Some people may need to use a wheelchair. Others may need a stick or crutches to support their walking. Standing and walking balance is also affected sometimes, causing the sufferer to be at risk of tripping and stumbling.

It is likely that your TM sufferer will have some problems with their bladder, bowel or sexual function. They may not want to talk about this, but naturally it affects their quality of life.

When a person discovers they may well never completely recover from a medical condition, it is understandable to fee "depressed" about it. With TM, however, there seems to be a physiological basis for more serious clinical depression.

Other symptoms may include paralysis, pain (different sorts), sensory impairment, numbness, pins and needles, headaches, backache.

SOME INFORMATION AND HELP

TMA website: www.myelitis,org
UK section of TMA website: www.myelitis.org.uk
Brain and spine foundation: www.brainandspine.org.uk
tel: 0808 808 1000

Neurological Alliance: www.neural.org.uk
For carers: www.carersonline.org
www.carersuk.org
www.crossroads.org

RADAR
Royal Association for
Disability & Rehabilitation   020 7250 3222
Information on benefits,
work, education, rights
motoring, leisure
For further info: www.direct.gov.uk
enter "disability" in your search engine
look for leaflets at your doctor's surgery
look in libraries
most large supermarkets and town centres

MOTABILITY   0800 093 10000

LAST WORD

This book is dedicated to my family, my friends, Jonathan for his company along the thorny way, Dr Cheetham for his great help and knowledge, Dr Adab my specialist, for giving her time and expertise, Anna and Lew and all members of the TM Society for the support, guidance and help, and to all who have helped me in this epic journey.

And lastly particular thanks and love to my carer-chauffeur-husband Jim, without whose help this book would not have been written, and without whom I would certainly not have coped.